Tiny Pyk

Curated Examples

MW00427029

Tiny Python 3.6 Notebook

Curated Examples

Matt Harrison

hairysun.com

COPYRIGHT © 2017

While every precaution has been taken in the
preparation of this book, the publisher and author
assumes no responsibility for errors or omissions, or for
damages resulting from the use of the information
contained herein

Contents

Contents

1 Introduction

This is not so much an instructional manual, but rather notes, tables, and examples for Python syntax. It was created by the author as an additional resource during training, meant to be distributed as a physical notebook. Participants (who favor the physical characteristics of dead tree material) could add their own notes, thoughts, and have a valuable reference of curated examples.

2   Running Python

2.1   Installation

To check if Python is installed, run the following from a terminal:

```
$ python3 --version
```

Otherwise, install Python 3 from the website[1].

2.2   Invoking Python

The Python executable will behave differently depending on the command line options you give it:

- Start the Python REPL:

  ```
  $ python3
  ```

- Execute the `file.py` file:

  ```
  $ python3 file.py
  ```

---

[1]http://python.org

- Execute the `file.py` file, and drop into REPL with namespace of `file.py`:

```
$ python3 -i file.py
```

- Execute the `json/tool.py` module:

```
$ python3 -m json.tool
```

- Execute `"print('hi')"`

```
$ python3 -c "print('hi')"
```

2.3 REPL

- Use the `help` function to read the documentation for a module/class/function. As a standalone invocation, you enter the help system and can explore various topics.

- Use the `dir` function to list contents of the namespace, or attributes of an object if you pass one in

Note

The majority of code in this book is written as if it were executed in a REPL. If you are typing it in, ignore the primary and secondary prompts (>>> and ...).

3   The Zen of Python

Run the following in an interpreter to get an Easter egg that describes some of the ethos behind Python. This is also codified in PEP 20:

```
>>> import this
The Zen of Python, by Tim Peters

Beautiful is better than ugly.
Explicit is better than implicit.
Simple is better than complex.
Complex is better than complicated.
Flat is better than nested.
Sparse is better than dense.
Readability counts.
Special cases aren't special enough to break the
rules.
Although practicality beats purity.
Errors should never pass silently.
Unless explicitly silenced.
In the face of ambiguity, refuse the temptation
to guess.
There should be one --and preferably only one--
obvious way to do it.
Although that way may not be obvious at first
unless you're Dutch.
Now is better than never.
Although never is often better than *right* now.
If the implementation is hard to explain, it's a
```

3. The Zen of Python

```
bad idea.
If the implementation is easy to explain, it may
be a good idea.
Namespaces are one honking great idea -- let's
do more of those!
```

These might just seem like silly one liners, but there is a lot of wisdom packed in here. It is good for Python programmers to review these every once in a while and see if these hold true for their code. (Or to justify their code reviews)

4 Built-in Types

4.1 Variables

Python variables are like cattle tags, they point to objects
(which can be classes, instances, modules, or functions),
but variables are not the objects. You can reuse variable
names for different object types (though you probably
shouldn't):

```
>>> a = 400    # a points to an integer
>>> a = '400'  # a now points to a string
```

> **Note**
>
> The # character denotes the start of a comment.
> There are no multi-line comments, though most
> editors with Python support can comment out a
> region.

The figure that follows illustrates how everything is an
object in Python and variables just point to them.

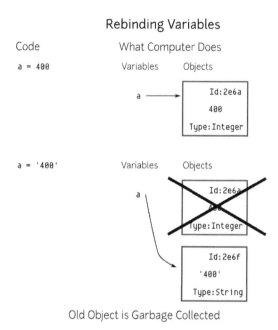

Rebinding Variables

Code

```
a = 400
```

```
a = '400'
```

Old Object is Garbage Collected

Figure 4.1: Illustration of reusing the same variable

4.2 Numbers

Python includes three types of numeric literals: *integers, floats,* and *complex numbers*. Python 3.6 adds the ability to use underscores to improve readability (PEP 515).

Type	Example
Integer	14
Integer (Hex)	0xe
Integer (Octal)	0o16
Integer (Binary)	0b1110
Float	14.0
Float	1.4e1
Complex	14+0j
Underscore	1_000

Table 4.1: Number types

There are many built-in functions for manipulating numbers ie. abs, min, max, ceil. Also see the math, random, and statistics modules in the standard library.

Operation	Provided By	Result
abs(num)	__abs__	Absolute value of num
num + num2	__add__	Addition
bool(num)	__bool__	Boolean conversion
num == num2	__eq__	Equality
float(num)	__float__	Float conversion
num // num2	__floordiv__	Integer division
num >= num2	__ge__	Greater or equal
num > num2	__gt__	Greater than
int(num)	__int__	Integer conversion
num <= num2	__le__	Less or equal

9

num < num2	__lt__	Less than
num % num2	__mod__	Modulus
num * num2	__mul__	Multiplication
num != num2	__ne__	Not equal
-num	__neg__	Negative
+num	__pos__	Positive
num ** num2	__pow__	Power
round(num)	__round__	Round
num.__sizeof__()	__sizeof__	Bytes for internal representation
str(num)	__str__	String conversion
num - num2	__sub__	Subtraction
num / num2	__truediv__	Float division
math.trunc(num)	__trunc__	Truncation

Table 4.2: Number magic methods

Operation	Provided By	Result
num & num2	__and__	Bitwise and
math.ceil(num)	__ceil__	Ceiling
math.floor(num)	__floor__	Floor
~num	__invert__	Bitwise inverse
num << num2	__lshift__	Left shift
num | num2	__or__	Bitwise or
num >> num2	__rshift__	Right shift
num ^ num2	__xor__	Bitwise xor
num.bit_length()	bit_length	Number of bits necessary

Table 4.3: Integer specific methods and operations

Operation	Result
f.as_integer_ratio()	Returns num, denom tuple
f.is_integer()	Boolean if whole number

Table 4.4: Float specific methods and operations

4.3 Strings

Python 3 strings hold unicode data. Python has a few ways to represent strings. There is also a bytes type (PEP 3137):

Type	Example
String	`"hello\tthere"`
String	`'hello'`
String	`'''He said, "hello"'''`
Raw string	`r'hello\tthere'`
Byte string	`b'hello'`

Table 4.5: String types

Operation	Provided By	Result
`s + s2`	`__add__`	String concatenation
`"foo" in s`	`__contains__`	Membership
`s == s2`	`__eq__`	Equality
`s >= s2`	`__ge__`	Greater or equal
`s[0]`	`__getitem__`	Index operation
`s > s2`	`__gt__`	Greater
`s <= s2`	`__le__`	Less than or equal
`len(s)`	`__len__`	Length
`s < s2`	`__lt__`	Less than
`s % (1, 'foo')`	`__mod__`	Formatting
`s * 3`	`__mul__`	Repetition
`s != s2`	`__ne__`	Not equal
`repr(s)`	`__repr__`	Programmer friendly string
`s.__sizeof__()`	`__sizeof__`	Bytes for internal representation
`str(s)`	`__str__`	User friendly string

4. Built-in Types

Table 4.6: String operations

Operation	Result
s.capitalize()	Capitalizes a string
s.casefold()	Lowercase in a unicode compliant manner
s.center(w, [char])	Center a string in w spaces with char (default " ")
s.count(sub, [start, [end]])	Count sub in s between start and end
s.encode(encoding, errors= 'strict')	Encode a string into bytes
s.endswith(sub)	Check for a suffix
s.expandtabs(tabsize=8)	Replaces tabs with spaces
s.find(sub, [start, [end]])	Find substring or return -1
s.format(*args, **kw)	Format string
s.format_map(mapping)	Format strings with a mapping
s.index(sub, [start, [end]])	Find substring or raise ValueError
s.isalnum()	Boolean if alphanumeric
s.isalpha()	Boolean if alphabetic
s.isdecimal()	Boolean if decimal
s.isdigit()	Boolean if digit
s.isidentifier()	Boolean if valid identifier
s.islower()	Boolean if lowercase
s.isnumeric()	Boolean if numeric

s.isprintable()	Boolean if printable
s.isspace()	Boolean if whitespace
s.istitle()	Boolean if titlecased
s.isupper()	Boolean if uppercased
s.join(iterable)	Return a string inserted between sequence
s.ljust(w, [char])	Left justify in w spaces with char (default ' ')
s.lower()	Lowercase
s.lstrip([chars])	Left strip chars (default spacing).
s.partition(sub)	Split string at first occurrence of substring, return (before, sub, after)
s.replace(old, new, [count])	Replace substring with new string
s.rfind(sub, [start, [end]])	Find rightmost substring or return -1
s.rindex(sub, [start, [end]])	Find rightmost substring or raise ValueError
s.rjust(w, [char)	Right justify in w spaces with char (default " ")
s.rpartition(sub)	Rightmost partition
s.rsplit([sep, [maxsplit=-1])	Rightmost split by sep (defaults to whitespace)
s.rstrip([chars])	Right strip
s.split([sep, [maxsplit=-1]])	Split a string into sequence around substring
s.splitlines(keep-ends=False)	Break string at line boundaries

`s.startswith(`
`  prefix,`
`  [start,`
`  [end]])`
	Check for prefix

`s.strip([chars])`	Remove leading and trailing whitespace (default) or `chars`
`s.swapcase()`	Swap casing of string
`s.title()`	Titlecase string
`s.translate(table)`	Use a translation table to replace strings
`s.upper()`	Uppercase
`s.zfill(width)`	Left fill with 0 so string fills `width` (no truncation)

Table 4.7: String methods

4.4 Lists

Lists are ordered mutable sequences:

```
>>> people = ['Paul', 'John', 'George']
>>> people.append('Ringo')
```

The `in` operator is useful for checking membership on sequences:

```
>>> 'Yoko' in people
False
```

If we need the index number during iteration, the `enumerate` function gives us a tuple of index, item pairs:

```
>>> for i, name in enumerate(people, 1):
...     print('{} - {}'.format(i, name))
1 - Paul
2 - John
3 - George
4 - Ringo
```

We can do index operations on most sequences:

14

```
>>> people[0]
'Paul'
>>> people[-1]  # len(people) - 1
'Ringo'
```

We can also do *slicing* operations on most sequences:

```
>>> people[1:2]
['John']
>>> people[:1]    # Implicit start at 0
['Paul']
>>> people[1:]    # Implicit end at len(people)
['John', 'George', 'Ringo']
>>> people[::2]   # Take every other item
['Paul', 'George']
>>> people[::-1]  # Reverse sequence
['Ringo', 'George', 'John', 'Paul']
```

Operation	Provided By	Result
l + l2	__add__	List concatenation (see .extend)
"name" in l	__contains__	Membership
del l[idx]	__del__	Remove item at index idx (see .pop)
l == l2	__eq__	Equality
"{}".format(l)	__format__	String format of list
l >= l2	__ge__	Greater or equal. Compares items in lists from left
l[idx]	__getitem__	Index operation
l > l2	__gt__	Greater. Compares items in lists from left
No hash	__hash__	Set to None to ensure you can't insert in dictionary
l += l2	__iadd__	Augmented (mutates l) concatenation

`l *= 3`	`__imul__`	Augmented (mutates l) repetition
`for thing in l:`	`__iter__`	Iteration
`l <= l2`	`__le__`	Less than or equal. Compares items in lists from left
`len(l)`	`__len__`	Length
`l < l2`	`__lt__`	Less than. Compares items in lists from left
`l * 2`	`__mul__`	Repetition
`l != l2`	`__ne__`	Not equal
`repr(l)`	`__repr__`	Programmer friendly string
`reversed(l)`	`__reversed__`	Reverse
`foo * l`	`__rmul__`	Called if foo doesn't implement `__mul__`
`l[idx] = 'bar'`	`__setitem__`	Index operation to set value
`l.__sizeof__()`	`__sizeof__`	Bytes for internal representation
`str(l)`	`__str__`	User friendly string

Table 4.8: List Operations

Operation	Result
`l.append(item)`	Append item to end
`l.clear()`	Empty list (mutates l)
`l.copy()`	Shallow copy
`l.count(thing)`	Number of occurrences of thing
`l.extend(l2)`	List concatenation (mutates l)
`l.index(thing)`	Index of thing else ValueError
`l.insert(idx, bar)`	Insert bar at index idx
`l.pop([idx])`	Remove last item or item at idx

l.remove(bar)	Remove first instance of bar else ValueError
l.reverse()	Reverse (mutates l)
l.sort([key=], re-verse=False)	In-place sort, by optional key function (mutates l)

Table 4.9: List Methods

4.5 Dictionaries

Dictionaries are mutable mappings of keys to values. Keys must be hashable, but values can be any object:

```
>>> instruments = {'Paul': 'Bass',
...                 'John': 'Guitar'}

>>> instruments['George'] = 'Guitar'
>>> 'Ringo' in instruments
False

>>> for name in instruments:
...     print('{} - {}'.format(name,
...           instruments[name]))
Paul - Bass
John - Guitar
George - Guitar
```

Operation	Provided By	Result
key in d	__contains__	Membership
del d[key]	__delitem__	Delete key
d == d2	__eq__	Equality. Dicts are equal or not equal
"{}".format(d)	__format__	String format of dict
d[key]	__getitem__	Get value for key (see .get)
for key in d:	__iter__	Iteration over keys
len(d)	__len__	Length
d != d2	__ne__	Not equal

17

repr(d)	__repr__	Programmer friendly string
d[key] = value	__setitem__	Set value for key
d.__sizeof__()	__sizeof__	Bytes for internal representation

Table 4.10: Magic Dictionary Methods

Operation	Result
d.clear()	Remove all items (mutates d)
d.copy()	Shallow copy
d.fromkeys(iter, value=None)	Create dict from iterable with values set to value
d.get(key, [default])	Get value for key or return default (None)
d.items()	View of (key, value) pairs
d.keys()	View of keys
d.pop(key, [default])	Return value for key or default (KeyError if not set)
d.popitem()	Return arbitrary (key, value) tuple. KeyError if empty
d.setdefault(k, [default])	Does d.get(k, default). If k missing, sets to default
d.update(d2)	Mutate d with values of d2 (dictionary or iterable of (key, value) pairs)
d.values()	View of values

Table 4.11: Dictionary Methods

4.6 Tuples

Tuples are immutable sequences. Typically they are used to store *record* type data:

```
>>> member = ('Paul', 'Bass', 1942)
>>> member2 = ('Ringo', 'Drums', 1940)
```

Note that parentheses aren't usually required:

```
>>> row = 1, 'Fred'      # 2 item tuple
>>> row2 = (2, 'Bob')    # 2 item tuple
>>> row3 = ('Bill')      # String!
>>> row4 = ('Bill',)     # 1 item tuple
>>> row5 = 'Bill',       # 1 item tuple
>>> row6 = ()            # Empty tuple
```

Named tuples can be used in place of normal tuples and allow context (or names) to be added to positional members. The syntax for creating them is a little different because we are dynamically creating a class first (hence the capitalized variable):

```
>>> from collections import namedtuple
>>> Member = namedtuple('Member',
...     'name, instrument, birth_year')
>>> member3 = Member('George', 'Guitar', 1943)
```

We can access members by position or name (name allows us to be more explicit):

```
>>> member3[0]
'George'
```

```
>>> member3.name
'George'
```

Operation	Provided	Result
t + t2	__add__	Tuple concatenation
"name" in t	__contains__	Membership
t == t2	__eq__	Equality
"{}".format(t)	__format__	String format of tuple

19

t >= t2	__ge__	Greater or equal. Compares items in tuple from left
t[idx]	__getitem__	Index operation
t > l2	__gt__	Greater. Compares items in tuple from left
hash(t)	__hash__	For set/dict insertion
for thing in t:	__iter__	Iteration
t <= t2	__le__	Less than or equal. Compares items in tuple from left
len(l)	__len__	Length
t < t2	__lt__	Less than. Compares items in tuple from left
t * 2	__mul__	Repetition
t != l2	__ne__	Not equal
repr(t)	__repr__	Programmer friendly string
foo * t	__rmul__	Called if foo doesn't implement __mul__
l.__sizeof__()	__sizeof__	Bytes for internal representation
str(l)	__str__	User friendly string

Table 4.12: Tuple Methods

Operation	Result
t.count(item)	Count of item
t.index(thing)	Index of thing else ValueError

Table 4.13: Tuple Methods

4.7 Sets

A set is a mutable unordered collection that cannot contain duplicates. Sets are used to remove duplicates and test for membership:

```
>>> digits = [0, 1, 1, 2, 3, 4, 5, 6,
...     7, 8, 9]
>>> digit_set = set(digits)   # remove extra 1

>>> 9 in digit_set
True
```

Sets are useful because they provide *set operations*, such as union (|), intersection (&), difference (-), and xor (^):

```
>>> odd = {1, 3, 5, 7, 9}
>>> prime = set([2, 3, 5, 7])
>>> even = digit_set - odd
>>> even
{0, 2, 4, 6, 8}

>>> prime & even  # in intersection
{2}

>>> odd | even    # in both
{0, 1, 2, 3, 4, 5, 6, 7, 8, 9}

>>> even ^ prime # not in both
{0, 3, 4, 5, 6, 7, 8}
```

Note

There is no literal syntax for an empty set. You need
to use:

```
>>> empty = set()
```

Operation	Provided By	Result
s & s2	__and__	Set intersection (see .intersection)
"name" in s	__contains__	Membership
s == s2	__eq__	Equality. Sets are equal or not equal
"{}".format(s)	__format__	String format of set
s >= s2	__ge__	s in s2 (see .issuperset)
s > s2	__gt__	Greater. Always False`
No hash	__hash__	Set to None to ensure you can't insert in dictionary
s &= s2	__iand__	Augmented (mutates s) intersection (see .intersection_update)
s |= s2	__ior__	Augmented (mutates s) union (see .update)
s -= s2	__isub__	Augmented (mutates s) difference (see .difference_update)
for thing in s:	__iter__	Iteration

`s ^= s2`	`__ixor__`	Augmented (mutates s) xor (see `.symmetric_difference_update`)
`s <= s2`	`__le__`	s2 in s (see `.issubset`)
`len(s)`	`__len__`	Length
`s < s2`	`__lt__`	Less than. Always `False`
`s != s2`	`__ne__`	Not equal
`s | s2`	`__or__`	Set union (see `.union`)
`foo & s`	`__rand__`	Called if foo doesn't implement `__and__`
`repr(s)`	`__repr__`	Programmer friendly string
`foo | s`	`__ror__`	Called if foo doesn't implement `__or__`
`foo - s`	`__rsub__`	Called if foo doesn't implement `__sub__`
`foo ^ s`	`__rxor__`	Called if foo doesn't implement `__xor__`
`s.__sizeof__()`	`__sizeof__`	Bytes for internal representation
`str(s)`	`__str__`	User friendly string
`s - s2`	`__sub__`	Set difference (see `.difference`)
`s ^ s2`	`__xor__`	Set xor (see `.symmetric_difference`)

Table 4.14: Set Methods

Operation	Result
s.add(item)	Add item to s (mutates s)
s.clear()	Remove elements from s (mutates s)
s.copy()	Shallow copy
s.difference(s2)	Return set with elements from s and not s2
s.difference_update(s2)	Remove s2 items from s (mutates s)
s.discard(item)	Remove item from s (mutates s). No error on missing item
s.intersection(s2)	Return set with elements from both sets
s.intersection_update(s2)	Update s with members of s2 (mutates s)
s.isdisjoint(s2)	True is there is no intersection
s.issubset(s2)	All elements of s in s2
s.issuperset(s2)	All elements of s2 in s2
s.pop()	Remove arbitrary item from s (mutates s). KeyError on missing item

`s.remove(item)`	Remove item from s (mutates s). KeyError on missing item
`s.symmetric_difference(s2)`	Return set with elements only in one of the sets
`s.symmetric_difference_update(s2)`	Update s with elements only in one of the sets (mutates s)
`s.union(s2)`	Return all elements of both sets
`s.update(s2)`	Update s with all elements of both sets (mutates s)

Table 4.15: Set Methods

5 Built in Functions

In the default namespace you have access to various callables:

Operation	Result
abs(x)	Absolute value protocol (call x.__abs__())
all(seq)	Boolean check if all items in seq are truthy
any(seq)	Boolean check if at least one item in seq is truthy
ascii(x)	ASCII representation of object
bin(i)	String containing binary version of number (int(bin(i), 2) to reverse)
bool(x)	Boolean protocol (call x.__bool__())
bytearray(x)	Create a mutable bytearray from iterable of ints, text string, bytes, an integer, or pass nothing for an empty bytearray
bytes(x)	Create an immutable bytes from iterable of ints, text string, bytes, an integer, or pass nothing for an empty bytes

`callable(x)`	Boolean check if you can do `x()` (ie `x.__call__` exists)
`chr(i)`	Convert integer codepoint to Unicode string (`ord(chr(i))` to reverse)
`@classmethod`	Use to decorate a method so you can invoke it on the class
`compile(source, fname, mode)`	Compile `source` to code (`fname` used for error, `mode` is `exec`: module, `single`: statement, `eval`: expression). Can run `eval(code)` on expression, `exec(code)` on statement
`complex(i, y)`	Create complex number
`copyright`	Python copyright string
`credits`	Python credits string
`delattr(obj, attr)`	Remove attribute from `obj` (`del obj.attr`)
`dict([x])`	Create a dictionary from a mapping, iterable of k,v tuples, named parameters, or pass nothing for an empty dictionary
`dir([obj])`	List attributes of `obj`, or names in current namespace if no `obj` provided
`divmod(num, denom)`	Return tuple pair of `num//denom` and `num%denom`
`enumerate(seq, [start])`	Return iterator of index, item tuple pairs. Index begins at `start` or `0` (default)
`eval(source, globals=None, locals=None)`	Run `source` (expression string or result of `compile`) with globals and locals
`exec(source, globals=None, locals=None)`	Run `source` (statement string or result of `compile`) with globals and locals

`exit(code)`	Exit Python interpreter and return code
`filter([function], seq)`	Return iterator of items where `function(item)` is truthy (or `item` is truthy if `function` is missing)
`float(x)`	Convert string or number to float (call `x.__float__()`)
`format(obj, fmt)`	Format protocol (call `obj.__format__(fmt)`)
`frozenset([seq])`	Create `frozenset` from `seq` (empty if missing)
`getattr(obj, attr)`	Get attribute from `obj` (`obj.attr`)
`globals()`	Return *mutable* dictionary with current global variables
`hasattr(obj, attr)`	Check if attribute on `obj` (`obj.attr` doesn't throw `AttributeError`)
`hash(x)`	Hash value protocol for object (call `x.__hash__()`)
`help([x])`	Start interactive help (if no x), or print documentation for x
`hex(i)`	String containing hexadecimal version of number (`int(hex(i), 16)` to reverse)
`id(x)`	Identity of x
`input([prompt])`	Read string from standard input
`int(x, [base=10])`	Create integer from number or string
`isinstance(obj, class_or_tuple)`	Boolean check if `obj` is an instance or subclass of `class_or_tuple`
`issubclass(cls, class_or_tuple)`	Boolean check if `cls` is the class or derived from `class_or_tuple`
`iter(seq)`	Iteration protocol (call `seq.__iter__()`)
`len(seq)`	Number of items in sequence

5. Built in Functions

`license()`	Display Python licenses
`list([seq])`	Convert seq to list (empty if missing)
`locals()`	Return dictionary of local attributes (unlike globals, not guaranteed to update namespace when mutated)
`map(function, *seqs)`	Call function(item) for item in seqs (if single sequence) or function(seqs[0][0], seqs[1][0]...)
`max(seq, *, [default], [key])`	Return maximum value from seq. default (value if empty seq) and key (function to determine magnitude) are keyword parameters.
`memoryview(obj)`	Create memoryview from obj
`min(seq, *, [default], [key])`	Return minimum value from seq. default (value if empty seq) and key (function to determine magnitude) are keyword parameters.
`next(iter, [default])`	Get next item from iteration protocol (call iter.__next__()), if default provide return instead of raising StopIteration
`object`	Root base type
`oct(i)`	String containing octal version of number (int(oct(i), 8) to reverse)
`open(filename, [mode], [encoding], [errors])`	Open a file

`ord(s)`	Convert Unicode string to integer codepoint (`chr(ord(s))` to reverse)
`pow(num, exp, [z])`	Power protocol (call `num.__pow__(exp, z)`)(`num ** exp` or `num ** exp % z`)
`print(val, [val2 ...], *, sep=' ', end='\n', file=sys.stdout)`	Print values to `file`. Print protocol (call `val.__str__()`)
`@property`	Decorator to turn a method into an attribute
`quit()`	Quit interpreter
`range([start], stop, [step])`	Return range object that iterates from `start` (default 0) to `stop` - 1, by `step` increments (default 1)
`repr(x)`	Representation protocol (call `x.__repr__()`)
`reversed(seq)`	Reverse iterator
`round(num, [ndigits=0])`	Round to `ndigits` protocol (call `num.__round__()`)
`set([seq])`	Create set from `seq` (empty if missing)
`setattr(obj, attr, val)`	Set attribute on `obj` (`obj.attr = val`)
`slice([start], stop, [step])`	Create `slice` object
`sorted(seq, * [key=None], [reverse=False])`	Sorted list in ascending order (use key function to customize sort property)
`@staticmethod`	Use to decorate a method so you can invoke it on the class or instance
`str(obj)`	Create string (call `obj.__str__()`)

`str(bytes, [encoding], [errors])`	Create string from bytes (`errors` defaults to `strict`)
`sum(seq, [start=0])`	Sum values from seq (use start as initial value)
`super()`	Get access to superclass
`tuple([seq])`	Convert seq to tuple (empty if missing)
`type(name, bases, dict)`	Create a new type of name, with base classes bases, and attributes dict
`type(obj)`	Return type of obj
`vars([obj])`	Return `obj.__dict__` or `locals()` if missing
`zip(seq1, [seq2, ...])`	Return iterable of tuples of (`seq1[0]`, `seq2[0]`), (`seq1[1]`, `seq2[1]`), ... until shortest sequence

Table 5.1: Built in callables

6 Unicode

Python 3 represents strings as Unicode. We can *encode* strings to a series of bytes such as UTF-8. If we have bytes, we can *decode* them to a Unicode string:

```
>>> x_sq = 'x²'
>>> x_sq.encode('utf-8')
b'x\xc2\xb2'

>>> utf8_bytes = b'x\xc2\xb2'
>>> utf8_bytes.decode('utf-8')
'x²'
```

If you have the unicode glyph, you can use that directly. Alternatively, you can enter a code point using \u followed by the 16-bit hex value xxxx. For larger code points, use \U followed by xxxxxxxx. If you have the Unicode name (obtained by consulting tables at unicode.org), you can use the \N syntax. The following are equivalent:

```
>>> result = 'x²'
>>> result = 'x\u00b2'
>>> result = 'x\N{SUPERSCRIPT TWO}'
```

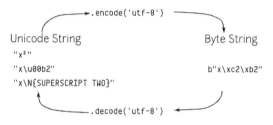

Figure 6.1: Image illustrating *encoding* a Unicode string to a byte representation. In this case, we convert to UTF-8. There are other byte encodings for this string. If we have a UTF-8 byte string, we can *decode* it into a Unicode string. Note that we should be explicit about the decoding as there are potentially other encodings that we could decode to that might give the user erroneous data, or *mojibake*.

7   String Formatting

Most modern Python code uses the `.format` method (PEP 3101) to create strings from other parts. The format method uses {} as a placeholder.

Inside of the placeholder we can provide different specifiers:

- {0} - reference first positional argument

- {} - reference implicit positional argument

- {result} - reference keyword argument

- {bike.tire} - reference attribute of argument

- {names[0]} - reference first element of argument

```
>>> person = {'name': 'Paul',
...     'instrument': 'Bass'}
>>> inst = person['instrument']

>>> print("Name: {} plays: {}".format(
...     person['name'], inst))
Name: Paul plays: Bass
```

or:

```
>>> print("Name: {name} "
...       "plays: {inst}".format(
...       name=person['name'], inst=inst))
Name: Paul plays: Bass
```

You can also use *f-strings* in Python 3.6 (see PEP 498):

```
>>> print(f'Name: {person["name"]} plays: {inst}')
Name: Paul plays: Bass
```

F-strings inspect variables that are available and allow you to inline methods, or attributes from those variables.

7.1 Conversion Flags

You can provide a *conversion flag* inside the placeholder.

- !s - Call str() on argument

- !r - Call repr() on argument

- !a - Call ascii() on argument

```
>>> class Cat:
...     def __init__(self, name):
...         self.name = name
...     def __format__(self, data):
...         return "Format"
...     def __str__(self):
...         return "Str"
...     def __repr__(self):
...         return "Repr"
>>> cat = Cat("Fred")
>>> print("{} {!s} {!a} {!r}".format(cat, cat, cat,
...       cat))
Format Str Repr Repr
```

7.2 Format Specification

You can provide a format specification following a colon. The grammar for format specification is as follows:

```
[[fill]align][sign][#][0][width][grouping_option]
[.precision][type]
```

The following table lists the field meanings.

Field	Meaning
fill	Fills in space with align
align	<-left align, >-right align, ^-center align, =-put padding after sign
sign	+-for all number, --only negative, *space*-leading space for positive, sign on negative
#	Prefix integers. 0b-binary, 0o-octal, 0x-hex
0	Enable zero padding
width	Minimum field width
grouping_option	,-Use comma for thousands separator, _-Use underscore for thousands separator
.precision	Digits after period (floats). Max string length (non-numerics)
type	s-string format (default) see Integer and Float charts

The tables below lists the various options we have for formatting integer and floating point numbers.

Integer Types	Meaning
b	binary
c	character - convert to unicode character
d	decimal (default)
n	decimal with locale specific separators
o	octal
x	hex (lower-case)
X	hex (upper-case)

Float Types	Meaning
e/E	Exponent. Lower/upper-case e
f	Fixed point
g/G	General. Fixed with exponent for large, and small numbers (g default)
n	g with locale specific separators
%	Percentage (multiplies by 100)

7.3 Some `format` Examples

Here are a few examples of using `.format`. Let's format a string in the center of 12 characters surrounded by *. * is the *fill* character, ^ is the *align* field, and 12 is the *width* field:

```
>>> "Name: {:*^12}".format("Ringo")
'Name: ***Ringo****'
```

Next, we format a percentage using a width of 10, one decimal place and the sign before the width padding. = is the *align* field, 10.1 are the *width* and *precision* fields, and % is the *float type*, which converts the number to a percentage:

```
>>> "Percent: {:=10.1%}".format(-44/100)
'Percent: -    44.0%'
```

Below is a binary and a hex conversion. The *integer type* field is set to b and x respectively:

```
>>> "Binary: {:#b}".format(12)
'Binary: 0b1100'

>>> "Hex: {:#x}".format(12)
'Hex: 0xc'
```

8 Files

The open function will take a file path and mode as input and return a file handle. There are various modes to open a file, depending on the content and your needs. If you open the file in binary mode, you will get bytes out. In text mode you will get strings back:

Mode	Meaning
'r'	Read text file (default)
'w'	Write text file (truncates if exists)
'x'	Write text file, throw FileExistsError if exists.
'a'	Append to text file (write to end)
'rb'	Read binary file
'wb'	Write binary (truncate)
'w+b'	Open binary file for reading and writing
'xb'	Write binary file, throw FileExistsError if exists.
'ab'	Append to binary file (write to end)

Table 8.1: File Modes

8.1 Writing Files

We use a context manager with a file to ensure that the file is closed when the context block exits.

41

```
>>> with open('/tmp/names.txt', 'w') as fout:
...     fout.write('Paul\r\nJohn\n')
...     fout.writelines(['Ringo\n', 'George\n'])
```

8.2 Reading Files

With an opened text file, you can iterate over the lines.
This saves memory as the lines are read in as needed:

```
>>> with open('/tmp/names.txt') as fin:
...     for line in fin:
...         print(repr(line))
'Paul\n'
'John\n'
'Ringo\n'
'George\n'
```

Operation	Result
f.__iter__()	Support iteration
f.__next__()	Return next item of iteration (line in text)
f.__repr__()	Implementation for repr(f)
f.buffer	File buffer
f.close()	Close file
f.closed	Is closed
f.detach()	Detach file buffer from file
f.encoding	The encoding of the file (default is locale.getpreferredencoding())
f.errors	Error mode of encoding ('strict' default)
f.fileno()	Return file descriptor
f.flush()	Write file buffer
f.isatty()	Is interactive file
f.linebuffering	Buffered by lines
f.name	Name of file
f.newlines	End of line characters encountered (tuple or string)

`f.read(size=-1)`	Read size characters (-1 is whole file)
`f.readable()`	Is opened for reading
`f.readline(size=-1)`	Read size characters from line (-1 is whole line)
`f.readlines(hint=-1)`	Read bytes less than hint characters of lines from file (-1 is all file)
`f.seek(cookie, whence=0)`	Change stream location to cookie bytes (may be negative) offset from whence (0 - start, 1 - current position, 2 - end).
`f.seekable()`	File supports random access
`f.tell()`	Current stream location
`f.truncate(pos=None)`	Truncate file to pos bytes
`f.writeable()`	File supports writing
`f.write(text)`	Write text to file
`f.writelines(lines)`	Write lines to file (provide newlines if you want them)

Table 8.2: File Methods

9 Functions

9.1 Defining functions

Functions may take input, do some processing, and return output. You can provide a docstring directly following the name and parameters of the function:

```
>>> def add_numbers(x, y):
...     """ add_numbers sums up x and y
...
...     Arguments:
...     x -- object that supports addition
...     y -- object that supports addition
...     """
...     return x + y
```

> **Note**
>
> We use whitespace to specify a block in Python. We typically indent following a colon. PEP 8 recommends using 4 spaces. Don't mix tabs and spaces.

We can create anonymous functions using the lambda statement. Because they only allow an expression following the colon, it is somewhat crippled in functionality.

They are commonly used as a `key` argument to `sorted`, `min`, or `max`:

```
>>> add = lambda x, y: x + y
>>> add(4, 5)
9
```

Functions can have *default* arguments. Be careful with mutable types here, as the default is bound to the function when the function is created, not when it is called:

```
>>> def add_n(x, n=42):
...     return x + n

>>> add_n(10)
52
>>> add_n(3, -10)
-7
```

Functions can support variable positional arguments:

```
>>> def add_many(*args):
...     result = 0
...     for arg in args:
...         result += arg
...     return result

>>> add_many()
0
>>> add_many(1)
1
>>> add_many(42, 3.14)
45.14
```

Functions can support variable keyword arguments:

```
>>> def add_kwargs(**kwargs):
...     result = 0
...     for key in kwargs:
...         result += kwargs[key]
...     return result

>>> add_kwargs(x=1, y=2, z=3)
6
```

```
>>> add_kwargs()
0

>>> add_kwargs(4)
Traceback (most recent call last):
    ...
TypeError: add_kwargs() takes 0 positional arguments
but 1 was given
```

You can indicate the end of positional parameters by
using a single ∗. This gives you keyword only parameters
(PEP 3102):

```
>>> def add_points(*, x1=0, y1=0, x2=0, y2=0):
...     return x1 + x2, y1 + y2

>>> add_points(x1=1, y1=1, x2=3, y2=4)
(4, 5)

>>> add_points(1, 1, 3, 4)
Traceback (most recent call last):
    ...
TypeError: add_points() takes 0 positional arguments
but 4 were given
```

9.2 Calling Functions

You can also use ∗ and ∗∗ to *unpack* sequence and
dictionary arguments:

```
>>> def add_all(*args, **kwargs):
...     """Add all arguments"""
...     result = 0
...     for num in args + tuple(kwargs.values()):
...         result += num
...     return result

>>> sizes = (2, 4.5)
>>> named_sizes = {"this": 3, "that": 1}
```

The following two examples are the equivalent:

```
>>> add_all(*sizes)
6.5

>>> add_all(sizes[0], sizes[1])
6.5
```

The following two examples are the equivalent:

```
>>> add_all(**named_sizes)
4

>>> add_all(this=3, that=1)
4
```

You can also combine $*$ and $**$ on invocation:

```
>>> add_all(*sizes, **named_sizes)
10.5
```

You can get help on a function that has a docstring by using help:

```
>>> help(add_all)
Help on function add_all in module __main__:

add_all(*args, **kwargs)
    Add all arguments
```

10 Classes

Python supports object oriented programming but doesn't require you to create classes. You can use the built-in data structures to great effect. Here's a class for a simple bike. The class attribute, num_passengers, is shared for all instances of Bike. The instance attributes, size and ratio, are unique to each instance:

```
>>> class Bike:
...     ''' Represents a bike '''
...     num_passengers = 1   # class attribute
...
...     def __init__(self, wheel_size,
...                  gear_ratio):
...         ''' Create a bike specifying the
...         wheel size, and gear ratio '''
...         # instance attributes
...         self.size = wheel_size
...         self.ratio = gear_ratio
...
...     def gear_inches(self):
...         return self.ratio * self.size
```

We can call the constructor (__init__), by invoking the class name. Note that self is the instance, but Python passes that around for us automatically:

```
>>> bike = Bike(26, 34/13)
>>> print(bike.gear_inches())
```

```
68.0
```

We can access both class attributes and instance attributes on the instance:

```
>>> bike.num_passengers
1

>>> bike.size
26
```

If an attribute is not found on the instance, Python will then look for it on the class, it will look through the parent classes to continue to try and find it. If the lookup is unsuccessful, an AttributeError is raised.

10.1 Subclasses

To subclass a class, simply place the parent class name in parentheses following the class name in the declaration. We can call the super function to gain access to parent methods:

```
>>> class Tandem(Bike):
...     num_passengers = 2
...
...     def __init__(self, wheel_size, rings, cogs):
...         self.rings = rings
...         self.cogs = cogs
...         ratio = rings[0] / cogs[0]
...         super().__init__(wheel_size, ratio)
...
...     def shift(self, ring_idx, cog_idx):
...         self.ratio = self.rings[ring_idx] \
...             / self.cogs[cog_idx]
...
```

> **Note**
>
> In the above example, we used a \ to indicate that
> the line continued on the following line. This is
> usually required unless there is an implicit line
> continuation with an opening brace that hasn't been
> closed ((, [, or {).

The instance of the subclass can call methods that are
defined on its class or the parent class:

```
>>> tan = Tandem(26, [42, 36], [24, 20, 15, 11])
>>> tan.shift(1, -1)
>>> tan.gear_inches()
85.0909090909091
```

10.2 Class Methods and Static Methods

The `classmethod` decorator is used to create methods
that you can invoke directly on the class. This allows us to
create alternate constructors. Note that the implicit first
argument is the class, commonly named `cls` (as `class` is
a keyword and will error out):

```
>>> INCHES_PER_METER = 39.37

>>> class MountainBike(Bike):
...     @classmethod
...     def from_metric(cls, size_meters, ratio):
...         return cls(size_meters *
...                    INCHES_PER_METER,
...                    ratio)


>>> mtn = MountainBike.from_metric(.559, 38/11)
>>> mtn.gear_inches()
76.0270490909091
```

> **Note**
>
> In the above example, we had an implicit line
> continuation without a backslash, because there was
> a (on the line.

The `staticmethod` decorator lets you attach functions to
a class. (I don't like them, just use a function). Note that
they don't get an implicit first argument. It can be called
on the instance or the class:

```
>>> class Recumbent(Bike):
...     @staticmethod
...     def is_fast():
...         return True

>>> Recumbent.is_fast()
True

>>> lawnchair = Recumbent(20, 4)
>>> lawnchair.is_fast()
True
```

10.3 Properties

If you want to have actions occur under the covers on
attribute access, you can use properties to do that:

```
>>> class Person:
...     def __init__(self, name):
...         self._name = name
...
...     @property
...     def name(self):
...         if self._name == 'Richard':
...             return 'Ringo'
...         return self._name
...
...     @name.setter
...     def name(self, value):
```

```
...          self._name = value
...
...      @name.deleter
...      def name(self):
...          del self._name
```

Rather than calling the `.name()` method, we access the attribute:

```
>>> p = Person('Richard')
>>> p.name
'Ringo'

>>> p.name = 'Fred'
```

11 Looping

You can loop over objects in a sequence:

```
>>> names = ['John', 'Paul', 'Ringo']
>>> for name in names:
...     print(name)
John
Paul
Ringo
```

The break statement will pop you out of a loop:

```
>>> for name in names:
...     if name == 'Paul':
...         break
...     print(name)
John
```

The continue statement skips over the body of the loop and *continues* at the next item of iteration:

```
>>> for name in names:
...     if name == 'Paul':
...         continue
...     print(name)
John
Ringo
```

You can use the else statement to indicate that every item was looped over, and a break was never encountered:

```
>>> for name in names:
...     if name == 'George':
...          break
... else:
...     raise ValueError("No Georges")
Traceback (most recent call last):
  ...
ValueError: No Georges
```

Don't loop over index values (range(len(names))). Use enumerate:

```
>>> for i, name in enumerate(names, 1):
...     print("{}. {}".format(i, name))
1. John
2. Paul
3. Ringo
```

11.1 while Loops

You can use while loops to create loops as well. If it is an infinite loop, you can break out of it:

```
>>> done = False
>>> while not done:
...     # some work
...     done = True
```

11.2 Iteration Protocol

To make an iterator implement __iter__ and __next__:

```
>>> class fib:
...     def __init__(self, limit=None):
...          self.val1 = 1
...          self.val2 = 1
...          self.limit = limit
...
```

```
...     def __iter__(self):
...         return self
...
...     def __next__(self):
...         val = self.val1
...         self.val1 = self.val2
...         self.val2 = val + self.val1
...         if self.limit is not None and \
...             val < self.limit:
...             return val
...         raise StopIteration
```

Use the iterator in a loop:

```
>>> e = fib(6)
>>> for val in e:
...     print(val)
1
1
2
3
5
```

Unrolling the protocol:

```
>>> e = fib(6)
>>> it = iter(e)    # calls e.__iter__()
>>> next(it)        # calls it.__next__()
1
>>> next(it)
1
>>> next(it)
2
>>> next(it)
3
>>> next(it)
5
>>> next(it)
Traceback (most recent call last):
  ...
StopIteration
```

12 Conditionals

Python has an `if` statement with zero or more `elif` statements, and an optional `else` statement at the end. In Python, the word `elif` is Dutch for *else if*:

```
>>> grade = 72

>>> def letter_grade(grade):
...     if grade > 90:
...         return 'A'
...     elif grade > 80:
...         return 'B'
...     elif grade > 70:
...         return 'C'
...     else:
...         return 'D'

>>> letter_grade(grade)
'C'
```

Python supports the following tests: >, >=, <, <=, ==, and !=. For boolean operators use and, or, and not (&, |, and ^ are the bitwise operators).

Note that Python also supports *range comparisons*:

```
>>> x = 4
>>> if 3 < x < 5:
...     print("Four!")
Four!
```

12. Conditionals

Python does not have a switch statement, often dictionaries are used to support a similar construct:

```
>>> def add(x, y):
...     return x + y

>>> def sub(x, y):
...     return x - y

>>> ops = {'+': add, '-': sub}

>>> op = '+'
>>> a = 2
>>> b = 3
>>> ops[op](a, b)
5
```

12.1 Truthiness

You can define the `__bool__` method to teach your classes how to act in a boolean context. If that doesn't exists, Python will use `__len__`, and finally default to `True`.

The following table lists *truthy* and *falsey* values:

Truthy	Falsey
True	False
Most objects	None
1	0
3.2	0.0
[1, 2]	[] (empty list)
{'a': 1, 'b': 2}	{} (empty dict)
'string'	"" (empty string)
'False'	
'0'	

13 Exceptions

Python can catch one or more exceptions (PEP 3110). You can provide a chain of different exceptions to catch if you want to react differently. A few hints:

- Try to keep the block of the `try` statement down to the code that throws exceptions

- Be specific about the exceptions that you catch

- If you want to inspect the exception, use as to create a variable to point to it

If you use a bare `raise` inside of an `except` block, Python's traceback will point back to the location of the original exception, rather than where it is raised from.

```
>>> def avg(seq):
...     try:
...         result = sum(seq) / len(seq)
...     except ZeroDivisionError as e:
...         return None
...     except Exception:
...         raise
...     return result

>>> avg([1, 2, 4])
```

```
2.3333333333333335

>>> avg([]) is None
True

>>> avg('matt')
Traceback (most recent call last):
  ...
TypeError: unsupported operand type(s) for +: 'int'
and 'str'
```

13.1 Raising Exceptions

You can raise an exception using the raise statement
(PEP 3109):

```
>>> def bad_code(x):
...     raise ValueError('Bad code')

>>> bad_code(1)
Traceback (most recent call last):
  ...
ValueError: Bad code
```

14 Decorators

A decorator (PEP 318) allows us to insert logic before and after a function is called. You can define a decorator with a function that takes a function as input and returns a function as output. Here is the identity decorator:

```
>>> def identity(func):
...     return func
```

We can decorate a function with it like this:

```
>>> @identity
... def add(x, y):
...     return x + y
```

A more useful decorator can inject logic before and after calling the original function. To do this we create a function inside of the function and return that:

```
>>> import functools
>>> def verbose(func):
...     @functools.wraps(func)
...     def inner(*args, **kwargs):
...         print("Calling with:{} {}".format(args,
...             kwargs))
...         res = func(*args, **kwargs)
...         print("Result:{}".format(res))
...         return res
...     return inner
```

Above, we use print functions to illustrate before/after behavior, otherwise this is very similar to identity decorator.

There is a special syntax for applying the decorator. We put @ before the decorator name and place that on a line directly above the function we wish to decorate. Using the @verbose line before a function declaration is syntactic sugar for re-assigning the variable pointing to the function to the result of calling the decorator with the function passed into it:

```
>>> @verbose
... def sub(x, y):
...     return x - y
```

This could also be written as, sub = verbose(sub). Note that our decorated function will still call our original function, but add in some print statements:

```
>>> sub(5, 4)
Calling with:(5, 4) {}
Result:1
1
```

14.1 Parameterized Decorators

Because we can use closures to create functions, we can use closures to create decorators as well. This is very similar to our decorator above, but now we make a function that will return a decorator. Based on the inputs to that function, we can control (or parameterize) the behavior of the decorator:

```
>>> def verbose_level(level):
...     def verbose(func):
...         @functools.wraps(func)
...         def inner(*args, **kwargs):
...             for i in range(level):  # parameterized!
...                 print("Calling with:{} {}".format(
...                     args, kwargs))
...             res = func(*args, **kwargs)
...             print("Result:{}".format(res))
...             return res
...         return inner
...     return verbose
```

When you decorate with parameterized decorators, the decoration looks differently, because we need to invoke the function to create a decorator:

```
>>> @verbose_level(2)
... def div(x, y):
...     return x/y

>>> div(1, 5)
Calling with:(1, 5) {}
Calling with:(1, 5) {}
Result:0.2
0.2
```

15 Class Decorators and Metaclasses

Python allows you to dynamically create and modify classes. Class decorators and metaclasses are two ways to do this.

15.1 Class Decorators

You can decorate a class definition with a *class decorator* (PEP 3129). It is a function that takes a class as input and returns a class.

```
>>> def add_chirp(cls):
...     'Class decorator to add speak method'
...     def chirp(self):
...         return "CHIRP"
...     cls.speak = chirp
...     return cls
...
>>> @add_chirp
... class Bird:
...     pass

>>> b = Bird()
>>> print(b.speak())
CHIRP
```

15.2 Creating Classes with type

You can use type to determine the type of an object, but you can also provide the name, parents, and attributes map, and it will return a class.

```
>>> def howl(self):
...     return "HOWL"

>>> parents = ()
>>> attrs_map = {'speak': howl}
>>> F = type('F', parents, attrs_map)

>>> f = F()
>>> print(f.speak())
HOWL
```

15.3 Metaclasses with Functions

In the class definition you can specify a metaclass (PEP 3115), which can be a function or a class. Here is an example of a function that can alter the class.

```
>>> def meta(name, parents, attrs_map):
...     def bark(self):
...         return "WOOF!"
...     attrs_map['speak'] = bark
...     return type(name, parents, attrs_map)

>>> class Dog(metaclass=meta):
...     pass

>>> d = Dog()
>>> print(d.speak())
WOOF!
```

15.4 Metaclasses with Classes

You can define a class decorator and use either `__new__` or `__init__`. Typically most use `__new__` as it can alter attributes like `__slots__`.

```
>>> class CatMeta(type): # Needs to subclass type
...     def __new__(cls, name, parents, attrs_map):
...         # cls is CatMeta
...         # res is the class we are creating
...         res = super().__new__(cls, name,
...             parents, attrs_map)
...         def meow(self):
...             return "MEOW"
...         res.speak = meow
...         return res
...
...     def __init__(cls, name, parents, attrs_map):
...         super().__init__(name, parents, attrs_map)

>>> class Cat(metaclass=CatMeta):
...     pass

>>> c = Cat()
>>> print(c.speak())
MEOW
```

16   Generators

Generators (PEP 255) are functions that suspend their state as you iterate over the results of them. Each yield statement returns the next item of iteration and then *freezes* the state of the function. When iteration is resumed, the function continues from the point it was frozen. Note, that the result of calling the function is a generator:

```
>>> def fib_gen():
...     val1, val2 = 1, 1
...     while 1:
...         yield val1
...         val1, val2 = val2, (val1+val2)
```

We can simulate iteration by using the iteration protocol:

```
>>> gen = fib_gen()
>>> gen_iter = iter(gen)
>>> next(gen_iter)
1
>>> next(gen_iter)
1
>>> next(gen_iter)
2
>>> next(gen_iter)
3
```

17   Coroutines

The asyncio library (PEP 3153) provides asynchronous I/O in Python 3. We use async def to define a *coroutine function* (see PEP 492). The result of calling this is a *coroutine object*. Inside a coroutine we can use var = await future to suspend the coroutine and wait for future to return. We can also await another coroutine. A coroutine object may be created but isn't run until an event loop is running:

```
>>> import asyncio
>>> async def greeting():
...     print("Here they are!")

>>> co = greeting()
>>> co  # Not running
<coroutine object greeting at 0x1087dcba0>

>>> loop = asyncio.get_event_loop()
>>> loop.run_until_complete(co)
Here they are!
>>> loop.close()
```

To return an object, use an `asyncio.Future`:

```
>>> async def compute(future):
...     print("Starting...")
...     # Simulate IO...
...     res = await answer()
...     future.set_result(res)

>>> async def answer():
...     await asyncio.sleep(1)
...     return 42

>>> f = asyncio.Future()
>>> loop = asyncio.get_event_loop()
>>> loop.run_until_complete(compute(f))
>>> loop.close()
>>> f.result()
42
```

> **Note**
>
> `await` and `async` are *soft keywords* in Python 3.6.
> You will get a warning if you use them for variable
> names. In Python 3.7, they will be reserved
> keywords.

> **Note**
>
> For backwards compatibility in Python 3.4:
>
> - await can be replaced with yield from
> - async def can be replaced with a function decorated with @asyncio.coroutine

17.1 Asynchronous Generators

Python 3.6 adds asynchronous generators (PEP 525). You can use the yield statement in an async def function:

```
>>> async def fib():
...     v1, v2 = 1, 1
...     while True:
...         # similate io
...         await asyncio.sleep(1)
...         yield v1
...         v1, v2 = v2, v1+v2
...         if v1 > 5:
...             break

>>> async def get_results():
...     async for num in fib():
...         print(num)

>>> loop = asyncio.get_event_loop()
>>> loop.run_until_complete(get_results())
1 # sleeps for 1 sec before each print
1
2
3
5
>>> loop.close()
```

18   Comprehensions

Comprehension constructs allow us to combine the functional ideas behind map and filter into an easy to read, single line of code. When you see code that is aggregating into a list (or dict, set, or generator), you can replace it with a list comprehension (or dict, set comprehension, or generator expression). Here is an example of the code smell:

```
>>> nums = range(10)
>>> result = []
>>> for num in nums:
...     if num % 2 == 0:  # filter
...             result.append(num*num)  # map
```

This can be specified with a list comprehension (PEP 202):

```
>>> result = [num*num for num in nums
...             if num % 2 == 0]
```

To construct a list comprehension:

- Assign the result (result) to brackets. The brackets signal to the reader of the code that a list will be returned:

  ```
  result = [ ]
  ```

- Place the *for* loop construct inside the brackets. No colons are necessary:

```
result = [for num in nums]
```

- Insert any operations that filter the accumulation after the for loop:

```
result = [for num in nums if num % 2 == 0]
```

- Insert the accumulated object (num*num) at the front directly following the left bracket. Insert parentheses around the object if it is a tuple:

```
result = [num*num for num in nums
          if num % 2 == 0]
```

18.1 Set Comprehensions

If you replace the [with {, you will get a set comprehension (PEP 274) instead of a list comprehension:

```
>>> {num*num for num in nums if num % 2 == 0}
{0, 64, 4, 36, 16}
```

18.2 Dict Comprehensions

If you replace the [with {, and separate the key and value with a colon, you will get a dictionary comprehension (PEP 274):

```
>>> {num:num*num for num in nums if num % 2 == 0}
{0: 0, 2: 4, 4: 16, 6: 36, 8: 64}
```

Note

In Python 3.6, dictionaries are now ordered by key entry. Hence the ordering above.

18.3 Generator Expressions

If you replace the [with (, you will get a generator instead of a list. This is called a *generator expression* (PEP 289):

```
>>> (num*num for num in nums if num % 2 == 0)
<generator object <genexpr> at 0x10a6f8780>
```

18.4 Asynchronous Comprehensions

Python 3.6 (PEP 530) gives us *asynchronous comprehensions*. You can add async following what you are collecting to make it asynchronous. If you had the following code:

```
>>> async def process(aiter):
...     result = []
...     async for num in aiter:
...         if num % 2 == 0:  # filter
...             result.append(num*num)  # map
```

You could replace it with:

```
>>> async def process(aiter):
...     result = [num*num async for num in aiter
...               if num % 2 == 0]
```

19   Context Managers

If you find code where you need to make sure something happens before *and* after a block, a context manager (PEP 343) is a convenient way to enforce that. Another code smell that indicates you could be using a context manager is a try/finally block.

Context managers can be created with functions or classes.

If we were writing a Python module to write TeX, we might do something like this to ensure that the environments are closed properly:

```
>>> def start(env):
...     return '\\begin{{{}}}'.format(env)

>>> def end(env):
...      return '\\end{{{}}}'.format(env)

>>> def may_error():
...     import random
...     if random.random() < .5:
...         return 'content'
...     raise ValueError('Problem')


>>> out = []
>>> out.append(start('center'))
```

```
>>> try:
...     out.append(may_error())
... except ValueError:
...     pass
... finally:
...     out.append(end('center'))
```

This code can use a context manager to be a little cleaner.

19.1   Function Based Context Managers

To create a context manager with a function, decorate with `contextlib.contextmanager`, and yield where you want to insert your block:

```
>>> import contextlib
>>> @contextlib.contextmanager
... def env(name, content):
...     content.append('\\begin{{{}}}'.format(name))
...     try:
...         yield
...     except ValueError:
...         pass
...     finally:
...         content.append('\\end{{{}}}'.format(name))
```

Our code looks better now, and there will always be a closing tag:

```
>>> out = []
>>> with env('center', out):
...     out.append(may_error())

>>> out
['\\begin{center}', 'content', '\\end{center}']
```

19.2 Class Based Context Managers

To create a class based context manager, implement the
__enter__ and __exit__ methods:

```
>>> class env:
...     def __init__(self, name, content):
...         self.name = name
...         self.content = content
...
...     def __enter__(self):
...         self.content.append('\\begin{{{}}}'.format(
...             self.name))
...
...     def __exit__(self, type, value, tb):
...         # if error in block, t, v, & tb
...         # have non None values
...         # return True to hide exception
...         self.content.append('\\end{{{}}}'.format(
...             self.name))
...         return True
```

The code looks the same as using the function based
context manager:

```
>>> out = []
>>> with env('center', out):
...     out.append(may_error())

>>> out  # may_error had an issue
['\\begin{center}', '\\end{center}']
```

19.3 Context objects

Some context managers create objects that we can use
while inside of the context. The open context manager
returns a file object:

```
with open('/tmp/test.txt') as fin:
    # muck around with fin
```

To create an object in a function based context manager, simply `yield` the object. In a class based context manager, return the object in the `__enter__` method.

20   Type Annotations

Python 3.6 (PEP 483 and 484) allows you to provide types for input and output of functions. They can be used to:

- Allow 3rd party libraries such as mypy[2] to run static typing

- Assist editors with type inference

- Aid developers in understanding code

Types can be expressed as:

> - Built-in classes
> - Third party classes
> - Abstract Base Classes
> - Types found in the `types` module
> - User-defined classes

A basic example:

---

[2]http://mypy-lang.org/

```
>>> def add(x: int, y: int) -> float:
...     return x + y

>>> add(2, 3)
5
```

Note that Python does not do type checking, you need to use something like mypy:

```
>>> add("foo", "bar")
'foobar'
```

You can also specify the types of variables with a comment:

```
>>> from typing import Dict
>>> ages = {}  # type: Dict[str, int]
```

20.1   The typing Module

This module allows you to provide hints for:

- Callback functions
- Generic containers
- The Any type

To designate a class or function to not type check its annotations, use the @typing.no_type_check decorator.

20.2   Type Checking

Python 3.6 provides no support for type checking. You will need to install a tool like mypy:

```
$ pip install mypy
$ python3 -m mypy script.py
```

21 Scripts, Packages, and Modules

21.1 Scripts

A script is a Python file that you invoke `python` on. Typically there is a line near the bottom that looks like this:

```
if __name__ == '__main__':
    # execute something
```

This test allows you to change the code path when you execute the code versus when you import the code. The `__name__` attribute of a module is set to `'__main__'` when you execute that module. Otherwise, if you import the module, it will be the name of the module (without `.py`).

21.2 Modules

Modules are files that end in `.py`. According to PEP 8, we lowercase the module name and don't put underscores between the words in them. Any module found in the `PYTHONPATH` environment variable or the `sys.path` list, can be imported.

21.3   Packages

A directory that has a file named __init__.py in it is a
package. A package can have modules in it as well as sub
packages. The package should be found in PYTHONPATH
or sys.path to be imported. An example might look like
this:

```
packagename/
  __init__.py
  module1.py
  module2.py
  subpackage/
    __init__.py
```

The __init__.py module can be empty or can import
code from other modules in the package to remove
nesting in import statements.

21.4   Importing

You can import a package or a module:

```
import packagename
import packagename.module1
```

Assume there is a fib function in module1. You have
access to everything in the namespace of the module you
imported. To use this function you will need to use the
fully qualified name, packagename.module1.fib:

```
import packagename.module1

packagename.module1.fib()
```

If you only want to import the fib function, use the
from variant:

```
from packagename.module1 import fib

fib()
```

You can also rename imports using as:

```
from packagename.module1 import fib as package_fib

package_fib()
```

22 Environments

Python 3 includes the venv module for creating a sandbox for your project or a *virtual environment*.

To create an environment on Unix systems, run:

```
$ python3 -m venv /path/to/env
```

On Windows, run:

```
c:\>c:\Python36\python -m venv c:\path\to\env
```

To enter or *activate* the environment on Unix, run:

```
$ source /path/to/env/bin/activate
```

On Windows, run:

```
c:\>c:\path\to\env\Scripts\activate.bat
```

Your prompt should have the name of the active virtual environment in parentheses. To *deactivate* an environment on both platforms, just run the following:

```
(env) $ deactivate
```

22.1 Installing Packages

You should now have a pip executable, that will install a package from PyPI[3] into your virtual environment:

```
(env) $ pip install django
```

To uninstall a package run:

```
(env) $ pip uninstall django
```

If you are having issues installing a package, you might want to look into alternative Python distributions such as Anaconda[4] that have prepackaged many harder to install packages.

---

[3]https://pypi.python.org/pypi

[4]https://docs.continuum.io/anaconda/

23　Note Area

24   Thanks

Thanks for your support. If you are interested in a free Python cheatsheet, please sign up for my mailing list at www.metasnake.com.